31 DAY WORKPLACE
Prayer
DEVOTIONAL
IN HIS PRESENCE

31 DAY WORKPLACE
Prayer
DEVOTIONAL
IN HIS PRESENCE

COLOSSIANS 3:23 WORK WILLINGLY AT WHATEVER YOU DO,
AS THOUGH YOU WERE WORKING FOR THE LORD RATHER FOR PEOPLE.

NICOLE PEPPERS

XULON PRESS

Xulon Press
2301 Lucien Way #415
Maitland, FL 32751
407.339.4217
www.xulonpress.com

Printed in the United States of America.

Edited by Xulon Press

ISBN-13: 9781545637838

Dedication

I want to dedicate this book to my Grandmother Marie Celestine, Aunt Georgia Ford, and Uncle Emory Celestine who taught me how to pray. It's through their legacy of prayer and faith that has sustained me over the years. I miss and love them dearly, and I dare not remove the landmarks that were set before me.

Jasmine, Jada, and Joshua my three precious jewels! True gifts from God. Thank you for being my prayer warriors and standing rear guard for mama. Thank you for allowing me the time to pray and write this book. Joshua thank you for being my accountability partner… Asking me weekly it seemed, how is your book coming along, lol. Jada thank you for being my prayer warrior and giving me worship music to keep relevant. Jasmine thank you for being a great example of leadership to Jada and Joshua. You have set the standard for this family and generations to come. I love you all and I thank God for giving me loving children, who desire to live a life of holiness. The three of you are destined for greatness and you will do mighty works in the Kingdom of God, in Jesus Name!

Acknowledgements

First, I want to thank The Lord who is the lover of my soul. He has restored me back to Him in such a way that my mind cannot comprehend. I live each day with an expectant heart, waiting to see what He will do next. I am overwhelmed by His love, and look forward to every new adventure!

Cheryl Latour Martin "Mama," I want to thank you for your strength! I witnessed you praying many nights for your children and many others. I would listen outside your bedroom door and hear you crying out as an intercessor. It taught me that Jesus was the source, and I watched you diligently seek him in prayer. Thank you for giving me such a rich legacy for me and my children. I love you!

Tommie Muhammad "Daddy," thank you for your determined spirit! You are forever challenging your children to live to their full potential, and to know who we are and where we come from. These are your words. Thank you for enriching us with our history and breaking the chains of generational defeat!

Ronald Martin "Papa," what can I say, you have been the wind beneath my wings, pushing me to fly! Thank you for not giving up on me, even when I wanted to give up on myself. Your love and support continue to be a blessing and a springboard to all the new adventures that lie ahead.

Reverend Ronnie LaTour, my anchor when I thought I was slipping. You have been a pillar of faith, strength, and love to our family. You never give up on one of God's people. You're forever determined to bring them to Christ…. Scriptures says forsake the 99 to go get the 1. I was the 1! You came to my rescue many of days. Your love guided me home, thank you!

Johnny & Shirley Smith, thank you for always seeing my way clear, being a true disciple of Jesus Christ. Never judging me, but always loving me, no matter my circumstance. I thank you for loving me and my children!

Bishop Shaun Cooper Sr. & Pastor Teresa Cooper of New Creation Family Church, thank you for being a demonstration of holiness in the body of Christ! I am in awe of your wonderful commitment to the work of ministry of Jesus Christ. You have served as mentors to me over the years, and guided me gently into the fold. I am forever grateful for your love and prayers!

Pastor John Peyton, I want to thank you for your ministry of reconciliation and your teachings. Reconciling me back to Christ. The moment I stepped in your church, I knew God was calling me back. I will never forget the Friday night service I visited because I knew my life would never be the same.

Minister Audrey Jones, and Ms. Frannie Weiland, thank you for the time when we spent every week for 2 years in intercessory prayer. You both taught me how to pray for others when I was going through a challenging time in my life. It was in our weekly, Thursday intercessory prayer that my relationship with Christ shifted. In 2010, my love for prayer was birthed in Woodbridge, Virginia. Thank you for taking the time to walk with me and to teach me how to intercede with power. My life has never been the same! I love you both.

Prophet Robert Washington, thank you for encouraging me to write this book. Your words of wisdom have pushed me toward my destiny! You are a true Prophet of God being used in the last days to set the captives free in the Kingdom of God!

Apostle Judy Brooks, thank you for speaking words of encouragement and pushing me to pursue my purpose. Your love and kindness has been a blessing to me and my children. I pray a double portion be added unto you and your ministry!

Introduction

————— ✦ —————

John 17:4 MSG

I glorified you on earth by completing down to the last detail what you assigned me to do.

I wrote this book out of obedience to the Lord. It was through my own personal experiences and struggles and hearing the burdens of others over the years that inspired me to write these daily prayers. There have been times that I would come home and pray earnestly for my colleagues, friends, and employees. My heart is for God's people to embrace their full potential while fulfilling their assignments given by God. These prayer devotionals are designed for leaders who desire to be fulfilled in their work. Whether you're an entrepreneur, teacher, manager, administrator, or executive, God has an assignment in the earth only you can complete. The key is believing in yourself. You must trust the process and cooperate with His plan allowing God to be your guide. Don't try and get ahead of Him. You must stay close to Him. Invite Christ into your work, into your heart, and into everything you do. Understand that it is Christ who equips you for every task that He purposed from the foundations of the earth.

I have questioned God about my role in my career path. Leadership can be challenging, frequently bringing out the worst or the best in you. My prayer has always been that the love of Christ would be revealed through my work. As an ambassador of Christ, I never want to misrepresent the Kingdom of God. But as *you know, we are not a perfect people, and we will make mistakes. I have worked in retail for most of my life, 20 years to be exact. In that time, I have been blessed to work under great leadership, with people who saw my capabilities before I did. There were also times of poor leadership that attempted to crush my spirit but God! I've seen how wrong intent and immoral thinking by leaders can cripple a person's professional and personal growth. We come to work stressed, allowing the fears of failure to grip us. Sometimes getting caught up in what people think, forgetting that we are here to serve others. What I have come to understand is that God has placed us in the workplace to bring the Kingdom of God.*

I recall a time years ago when I was newly promoted to a multi-unit manager. I was young and eager to learn and grow. The company was going through a transition and I was instrumental in assisting with the transition. The leadership was wonderful, and I worked with a great team of multi-unit managers. Professionally, this was one of the best and worst times of my life. Yes, I said best and worst. Let me explain what I mean. During this time, I grew professionally, but I had some internal struggles. My leader served as a mentor to the team. He led by serving others and with integrity. Our team was considered the dream team of retail. Others in the company envied the leadership and the cohesiveness of our team. I recognized that I was a part of something special, but I was unable to fully embrace it. While others on the team flourished, I seemed to withdraw.

Privately, I struggled with loneliness, fear, and rejection. Even though I was blessed to receive this awesome opportunity to lead I lacked confidence. I did not know my purpose. And because of that, my career began to suffer, not to mention my team. This was difficult because I had a leader who believed in me and a team that supported me, but I did not believe in myself. Both areas of my life were crumbling around me. I did not know what to do. No one knew about my internal struggles, so I was unable to confide in anyone. My own personal pride, shame, and fear of disappointing family and friends kept me in silence. But deep down inside I cried out to God for help. One afternoon in the guest room of my home I knelt in prayer, and gave my life to Christ. I didn't want to live in fear anymore. I wanted to know my purpose, I wanted to fulfil my purpose, and I wanted to lead with purpose. That day I was filled with the power of the Holy Spirit. It was beautiful and sweet. Jesus touched my heart! He healed me and set me free! I began to move forward, learning along the way that God has a specific plan for each of us. Our responsibility is not to get distracted but to pursue God's will for our life.

There are several behaviors that I have seen distract people from fulfilling God's purpose in the workplace and in their personal lives. People pleasing, power, position, greed, and fear. All of these behaviors work against a person's full potential. It can distract them from seeing or receiving the promises of God. God expects us to work willingly unto Him. Putting aside self and pursuing His will. He places us in our position, and there is an expectation, and the expectation requires our response. How we respond determines our success or failure. It determines the ultimate purpose, which is for Christ to be present in our daily lives. Yes, even while we are at work. Our obedience to His purpose determines His presence. One way I was able to invite His presence in my work was through prayer. It taught me how to understand and value my contribution to the organization. You must know who you are in Christ to know your value. If you lack understanding in this area, you may struggle to gain buy-in and commitment from people. Finding yourself always vying for attention or even competing, rather than serving. Christ came, and He led, but He first served. He chose to serve while leading, never competing, or looking for promotion.

Christ knew His value and He understood His purpose. He wants the same for us. Christ wants to promote you. He wants to open doors that no man can shut. He wants to give you tools to live by faith. But most of all, He wants you to bring the Kingdom of God into your daily environment, where joy and love is your portion! I hope these prayers inspire you to see your potential through the lenses of Christ and stretch your faith to new heights. God has prepared a life of purpose, filled with unlimited possibilities just for you! I would encourage you to start your day in prayer, followed by reflection. Allow the Holy Spirit to speak to you and lead all your decisions for the day. You will begin to see your purpose come alive!

Day 1

Colossians 3:23 NLT

Work willingly at whatever you do, as though you were working for the Lord rather for people.

"His Divine Purpose"

Today I pray…

Father, I thank You for allowing me to have employment. It's by your divine promise and love for me that you have given me a specific work assignment. Help me to know your will and purpose for my life. I do not want to work to please man, but to please my Father. As I go out in my day, help me to see your hand in all that I do. I bind ever negative spirit that would manipulate my thoughts causing me to desire money, power, or position. Help me to see that you have placed me here to be a blessing. To add value to my employer. To walk in humility and not pride. To be a representative of the Kingdom of God. To respond to all You ask me to do appropriately, not thinking of self, but that your will be done and Your purpose fulfilled. In Jesus Name, Amen.

Reflection_____

_____

_____

Day 2

Ephesians 6:6-7 NLT

Try to please them all the time, not just when they are watching you. As slaves of Christ, do the will of God with all your heart. Work with enthusiasm, as though you were working for the Lord rather than for people.

"A Representative of Christ"

Today I pray….

Father, I thank You for reminding me of my responsibility to work with a cheerful heart. I do not complain or get entangled in things at work that are not pleasing to You. I come against every attack of the enemy that will attempt to cause me to be unproductive within my organization. Father, I choose to work with joy being the center of all my work assignments. I spread the love of Christ in the workplace, not to be seen, but to be felt. Your spirit in me changes the atmosphere in my work environment. There is productivity, creativity, collaboration, all working harmoniously together. You are my Lord, and I live to serve you daily. It is through your grace that I have the gift to distribute your joyous love throughout the earth It is my heart's desire to bring light where darkness may dwell. To bring joy where sadness rules, unity where division settles, and peace where contention lives. I pray all these things In Jesus Mighty Name, Amen.

*Reflection*_____

_____

_____

Day 3

1 Peter 4:10 NLT

God has given each of you a gift from his great variety of spiritual gifts. Use them well to serve one another.

"A Servant Heart"

Today I pray…

Father, I thank You this day for your unyielding love towards me. I thank you that you came to show us how to serve and love one another without complaint. Not to be selfish, but to walk with a servant's heart, adding value to those whom I work with. Father, I come to you asking in your mighty name to teach me how to serve my leader, colleagues, and customers with authentic servitude. You are the master teacher; you teach all things, and you make all things new. Open my heart to receive your gift of servitude. Allow me to walk in the anointing of a servant, without complaints, but with a loving spirit, desiring to please the Father and to do His will in the workplace. Open my eyes to all the spiritual gifts that are inside me, and help me to recognize them to be able to serve your people. I refuse to become a snare in the enemy's trap to rob me of your great commission to serve one another. But I choose to follow your leading with my spirit open to receive all you have desired for me this day and forever more. I thank you Holy Spirit, for living inside me and teaching me how to be more like Christ. I shall go forth this day and lead, by serving others, In Jesus Mighty Name, Amen.

*Reflection*_____

_____

_____

Day 4

Isaiah 22:22 NLT

I will give him the key to the house of David—the highest position in the royal court. When he opens doors, no one will be able to close them; when he closes doors, no one will be able to open them.

"Step by Step"

Today I pray...

Father, thank You for promotion. I understand that all my promises are sealed in You, and You hold the keys. I can do nothing separate from You. Help me to understand that I must walk with a sincere heart in the workplace. You have positioned me in this season to be a distributor of Your good works. Allow Your purpose to be fulfilled through me with a spirit of excellence. I accept leadership at all levels and desire to please You in my assignment. I bind the spirit of entitlement, and I release the spirit of humility. Help me to embrace challenges that come up in the workplace with a humble heart, so that I can be a leader of change. I know that every good thing you have for me will be distributed in its proper time. The doors that You have opened cannot be shut! I will recognize the opportunities that You place before me and move forward with a thankful spirit, In Jesus Name, Amen.

*Reflection*_____

_____

_____

Day 5

---◆---

Psalm 94:18-19 KJV

I cried out, "I am slipping!" but your unfailing love, O Lord, supported me. When doubts filled my mind, your comfort gave me renewed hope and cheer.

"Continual Trust"

Today I pray…

Father, thank You for catching me when I feel like I am slipping. I know You have me in the palm of Your hands. There is no assignment too great for me to complete. You guide me with skillful hands and You teach me with guided wisdom. Allow me to feel Your presence right now. Shield me from the adversary of fear. Allow courage to take root in my heart this day. I have no doubts in me, and I reject the spirit of failure and defeat. You make me victorious in my work. I add value to those under my leadership. I bring courage into all assignments given to me and my team. I lead with the heart of a lion! It is You that gives me hope when I feel like I am slipping. It is You Lord that comforts me when results are not there. I thank You Lord for renewing my strength and for helping me to walk in what I cannot see. I believe that all tasks that are before me are complete and victorious in Jesus Name. I decree and declare that today my hope will be renewed in You, In Jesus Mighty Name, Amen.

Reflection_____

_____

_____

Day 6

Isaiah 54:2 KJV

Enlarge the place of thy tent, and let them stretch forth the curtains of thine habitations: spare not, lengthen thy cords, and strengthen thy stakes;

"Expansion through Strength"

Today I pray…

Father, thank You for stretching me and lengthening every good work that You have positioned for me and my employees. Let my heart rejoice because You have strengthened Your people this day and established greatness in Your purpose. I remain grounded in the purpose of Your will. My stakes are rooted deep in Your love. Allow my leadership to bring the strength of Your stakes into the workplace, where Your cords can be lengthened in Your people. I thank You that You have assigned me to pull back the curtains of financial profitability. You have given me the leadership authority to speak over every financial document that is attached to my team, in Jesus Name. I thank You for enlarging my financial territory and cancelling all deficits. What was in the red is now in the black, and what was a loss is now a gain. You have given me strategies to cover occupied financial territories connected to me. You have enlarged my entire team's profitability in the Kingdom of Heaven. You have given me the support to carry the weight of my team's financial responsibility. My stakes are in the ground, in Jesus Name, Amen.

*Reflection*_____

_____

_____

Day 7

Ephesians 4:29 KJV

Let no corrupt communication proceed out of your mouth, but that which is good to the use of edifying, that it may minister grace unto the hearers.

"Holy Spirit Speak"

Today I pray…

Father, I thank You for providing me with good communication skills. I want to connect with my employees on a level that brings clarity and understanding. Allow my words to be as sweet as a honeycomb, allowing each individual to hear the voice of God through me. Let not my speech be negative, nor my words be words of complaint. I see the blessings of communicating with purpose; it brings positive results, and it blesses the hearer. I denounce all communication that is not productive for me or my team. I bind all communication that creates strife, confusion, or distrust within my team. And I release the spirit of harmony, peace, and unity. You have placed me in this organization to demonstrate effective communication through Christ. Allow your grace to be received this day, in Jesus Name, Amen.

*Reflection*_____

_____

_____

7

Day 8

Colossians 3:15 ESV

Let the peace of Christ rule in your hearts, since as members of one body you were called to peace. And be thankful.

"Peace Maker"

Today I pray...

Father, I thank You for ruling and reigning in my heart. It is my desire to lead my team according to Your will. I submit my thoughts unto You, and trust that You will instruct me this day. My desire is to submit to Your plans for the day and the assignment that You have equipped for me to accomplish. I choose to work in peace and not let frustration be in my environment. You have given me the authority, through the Holy Spirit, to create an atmosphere that brings peace. I reject anything that will attempt to interfere with my peace. I understand that it is through the peace of God that I find joy and fulfillment in my work. I am thankful that You are mindful of me and that You have called me to peace. It's in peace that Your presence can be felt and where I draw my greatest strength. I ask today that You bless my team with peace. Let every concern they have be washed by Your precious blood. I bind any distractors that will attempt to thwart Your plans for my team. I am thankful that You are my guide and anchor. I rest in You, in Jesus Name, Amen

Reflection_____

_____

_____

Day 9

Matthew 6:27 NLT

*Can all your worries add a single
moment to your life?*

"Free from Worry"

Today I pray…

*Father, I thank You for teaching me how not to worry because
when I worry I am not trusting You. I denounce worry in Jesus
Name! Worry has no place in my heart because faith resides there.
It's through my faith that I can accomplish whatever the day may
bring. I know it's Your will for me to be successful, so I choose
not to worry about anything. You're my rock, my shield, and my
fortress in the day of trouble. Whom shall I fear? No one because
you have placed me in Your perfect position. When I find myself
drifting off into negative thoughts, I will remind myself how much
You love me. I will be the encourager, guiding my team toward the
finish line. Lord, I thank You for teaching me how to lead without
worry. I know defeat is nowhere in sight because You have called
me to victory. You have called me to success and You have called
me to lead, in Jesus Name, Amen*

Reflection_____

_____

_____

Day 10

Psalm 139:5 KJV

*Thou hast beset me behind and before,
and laid thine hand upon me.*

"Surrounded by God's Love"

Today I pray…

Father, I thank You for Your hands being upon me and Your eyes always fixed on me. You know my coming and my going. It is Your love that covers me. I know that You want nothing but the best for me. I submit to Your will and purpose. Thank You for guiding me throughout the day. I purpose to be a leader that will lead by example, knowing that You are beside me. Thank You for gifting me to move in the spirit of excellence. All my work projects are complete and received with approval, in Jesus Name. My team will finish their assignments and meet every deadline without any distractions. Thank You for placing Your hand upon this organization We are blessed with financial prosperity because of Your faithfulness. Our customers are referring and returning to purchase with us. I thank You for allowing me to serve in this season with a wonderful team of professionals, in Jesus Name, Amen

*Reflection*_____

_____

_____

Day 11

Proverbs 3:19 KJV

The Lord by wisdom hath founded the earth; by understanding hath he established the heavens.

"Knowledge of Christ"

Today I pray…

Father, I thank You for Your wisdom and understanding. Through You, all things become possible. Today, I choose to believe for greater. My faith is rooted in You. You make all things new. The creator of the heavens and the earth is guiding me through every circumstance. I will not focus on things that I cannot control, but instead, remain faithful in Your promises. Every word You have spoken has been established in the heavens. I thank You that I have access to those words. Words of peace, love, and hope. I will be a distributor of Your word in the workplace. Offering hope, when despair arises. Ensuring peace and denouncing confusion. Giving love, when harmony has been lost. Wisdom will guide me today in Jesus Name, Amen.

Reflection_____

_____

_____

Day 12

James 4:10 KJV

*Humble yourselves in the sight of
the Lord, and he shall lift you up.*

"Yielding to Love"

Today I Pray…

Father, I thank You for giving me a heart of humility. I know that it is Your will for me to lead with a compassionate heart. It is only through the heart that we can truly lead and guide others. Father, I humble myself before You and all that You have purposed for my life. Today, I choose to seek out every good thing that will draw me closer to You and Your will. You are the lifter of my soul, and I shall rejoice! I will look to the hills which cometh my help, and all my help comes from You. I shall be the encourager who leads people to a greater understanding of their purpose. I acknowledge that You have placed me in this organization not by accident but by design. You specifically chose to use me to demonstrate humility so that Christ can be revealed in the workplace. I thank You for opening my eyes of understanding and teaching me Your ways. I humble myself before You this day, receiving all that You have purposed for me to do in this organization. Thank You for guiding and using me to be the example of Your great love. There is no greater assignment than the assignment set before me this day in Jesus Name, Amen

Reflection_____

_____

_____

Day 13

Proverbs 11:3 KJV

The integrity of the upright shall guide them: but the perverseness of transgressors shall destroy them.

"The Path of Righteousness"

Today I pray…

Father, I thank You that I walk in Your integrity and it guides me. You're my navigator that charts my course. When I am faced with difficult situations, I turn to You for wisdom and guidance. I will not stumble. I will remain steadfast in my pursuit to always do the right thing. It's my desire to please You Lord. I remember Your word that is hidden in my heart. I will not be distracted by unexpected challenges that may arise, but I will remain focused on the truth of Your promises. Promises of peace, joy, prosperity, and faithfulness. I am committed to walking with a pure heart and a desire to make the right choices for my team and organization. I will continually look to You to navigate my thoughts and purify my heart, clearing the path for righteousness to prevail, in Jesus Name, Amen.

*Reflection*_____

_____

_____

Day 14

Romans 8:33 KJV

*Who shall lay anything to the charge of
God's elect? It is God that justifieth.*

"God Chooses"

Today I pray…

*Father, I thank You for positioning me within my organization. It is by
Your great hand that I am given this opportunity to lead. You have
chosen me, and You have justified all my steps! Who shall come
against the work of The Lord? Every responsibility that is given to
me has Your seal of approval and I shall not fail but succeed. I thank
You for aligning me with others who carry the same mantle of leadership.
You have given us access to bring the kingdom of God to
the workplace, where Your light can shine brightly before ALL men.
I thank You that there are no roadblocks for what You have called
Your leaders to accomplish in this season. Your hands are upon
those who seek to do Your will and only Your will. It is by Your grace
and mercy that we have been given the opportunity to lead. Who
shall come against God's chosen? Father, I thank You for Your protection.
I fear not, and I hold claim to Your promises. I thank You that
I am aligned with You in the spirit. I follow Your voice, and I listen for
Your direction. I do not entertain the thoughts of failure, but I explore
the thoughts of success. I do not seek man's approval, but I desire
to please You. Thank You for victory over everything that is assigned
to me. I trust and know that it is You who has graciously qualified
me to lead. There is no weapon that shall be formed against Your
great hand. You have chosen me this day, in Jesus Name, Amen.*

Reflection_____

_____

Day 15

Isaiah 50:4 NCV

The Lord God gave me the ability to teach so that I know what to say to make the weak strong. Every morning he wakes me. He teaches me to listen like a student.

"Communicating with God's Voice"

Today I Pray…

Father, I thank You, for You have made me an effective communicator. I speak as the learned and I connect with my audience. You have given me the ability to make change through my communication. You have given me the ability to discern accurately to ensure that I make the right decisions for my organization and my employees. You have equipped me with the ability to encourage those who are weary. I thank You that You continuously teach me day by day how to hear Your voice. You said You would never leave me nor forsake me. I thank You Father for Your unyielding love. I will walk boldly this day, knowing that You are the master teacher and I, the student. Teach me Lord and I will listen. As Samuel said, "Here I am." I say, "Here I am" Lord, in Jesus Name, Amen.

*Reflection*_____

_____

_____

Day 16

Revelation 3:8 NKJV

I know your works. See, I have set before you an open door, and no one can shut it; for you have a little strength, have kept My word, and have not denied My name.

"The Open Door"

Today I Pray…

Father, I thank You, for You know everything about me, and have not forsaken me. It is in Your everlasting love that You have opened every door to my future. You have placed me in a position of abundance. There are many doors before me and I choose to walk through every opportunity that You place before me. All doors of the enemy are closed and sealed with the blood of Jesus upon the door post. I thank You, for in my weakness, You make me strong. I refuse to give into the pressures of my daily assignments, but I choose to lift Your name on high. The Kingdom of God will not be denied in the workplace, but it shall be lifted this day. Thank You for trusting me with greater responsibilities to lead. Every new door brings greater insight of who You are in my life and the impact I have in my organization. Today, I chose to walk through the open door made available through Your love, in Jesus Name, Amen.

*Reflection*_____

_____

_____

Day 17

Acts 2:25 NLT

I see that the Lord is always with me. I will not be shaken, for he is right beside me.

"Never Alone"

Today I Pray…

Father, I thank You that I am never alone for You are always with me. Every challenge is a greater opportunity for my faith to be stretched. Thank You for setting this journey before me and traveling the road with me. I ask in Jesus Name that You strengthen and teach me how not to be shaken by unrighteousness in the workplace. Help me to pray always for salvation and deliverance, putting aside judgement and releasing love into the atmosphere. I bind every attack of the enemy that comes to destroy my peace at work. If You are for me, then who can stand against me? No one! I praise God for Your righteous hand upon me. I thank You for equipping me to stand in all situations whether great or small. For I know I will not be moved out of position because You have called me to this place. You have secured me in this assignment. I will finish what You have instructed me to complete in this season in Jesus Name, Amen.

*Reflection*_____
_____
_____

Day 18

Proverbs 12:24 NIV

Diligent hands will rule, but laziness ends in forced labor.

"Active in God"

Today I Pray...

Father, I thank You that laziness can't rule my atmosphere. I work with diligence. I walk in obedience to what You have instructed me to do this day. I refuse to give into complacent behaviors but choose to rise to every occasion and be a finisher. I thank You for giving me the authority to rule my environment. It is in my authority given by You, that I speak productivity to be active all around me. I decree and declare that my team is productive in Jesus Name. Laziness has no place in my life. I will continually seek opportunities to grow spiritually and professionally. I will not be distracted by things that have no value for myself or my organization. I choose to work in liberty, not constrained to unproductive labor. Thank You Jesus for making me a person with skillful hands that takes pleasure in their work. I embrace every assignment with joy and receive every challenge as an opportunity for You to be glorified in Jesus Name, Amen.

Reflection_____

_____

_____

Day 19

1 Peter 5:7 NIV

*Cast all your anxiety on him
because he cares for you.*

"Boldness in Christ"

Today I pray...

Father, thank You for giving me a courageous heart. I know that You love me and will never leave me. It is through Your love that I remain strong and not fearful. I seek You out daily, for You are my solid rock. You are my strong tower which cannot be breached. It is through Your love that You placed me in the palm of Your hand. I will not be moved. I know that You care for me and the vision You gave for my life. I lean not to my own understanding, but I choose to acknowledge and give You praise for what You are doing in and through me. I say today that fear, anxiety, and worry must go! As a leader, I take position and authority over every area of my life. Defeat has no space. My territory is expanded in Your victory. I walk in total victory in the workplace, in my community, and at home. Thank You Father for loving me and always guiding me to Your place of refuge. A place where peace lives and love reigns. I go forth this day like the Lion of Judah, strong and mighty! Walking boldly and fiercely, loving all those around me, in Jesus Name, Amen.

*Reflection*_____

_____

_____

Day 20

Numbers 27:18 NIV

So, the Lord said to Moses, "Take Joshua son of Nun, a man in whom is the spirit of leadership, and lay your hand on him.

"The Anointing"

Today I Pray…

Father, thank You, for You have anointed me for leadership. It is Your hands that rest upon my life. You created me to lead. You called me by name for this very hour. I embrace this assignment with joy. For the joy of The Lord is my strength! Father thank You for Your continued guidance. It is Your Word that sustains me in all situations. All my steps are ordered by You. I take each step with confidence that I am heading in the right direction. My team is headed in the right direction because You have given me insight into our journey. Our journey is victorious because You are victory! As I go forth this day, may Your hand continually be upon me for good works unto You, in Jesus Name, Amen.

*Reflection*_____

_____

_____

Day 21

Proverbs 19:21 NLT

*You can make many plans, but the
Lord's purpose will prevail.*

"The Plan of God"

Today I pray…

*Father, thank You, for Your plans are always good before me. I do
not lean unto my own understanding, but I hold fast to Your truth.
Your blueprint lays before me. I see clearly, and I hear Your voice
directing me this day. I see the intricate lines that are drawn out
before me for success. I rejoice because Your plans never fail.
What You have purposed for me is revealed in my obedience to
Your Word. I take pleasure in seeking out Your purpose for me and
my organization. You have strategically outlined what will be and
what is to come. Your plans are always designed with purpose. It's
purpose that allows victory to prevail! I surrender all my plans to
You this day. I take hold of all Your ideas, promises, and instruc-
tions. I give way to new thinking patterns, breaking old mindsets.
I choose to have the mind of Christ which elevates my thinking. I
choose to live in the transformation of Your spirit, embracing Your
plans, and living in Your purpose this day, in Jesus Name, Amen.*

Reflection_____

_____

_____

Day 22

Isaiah 43:2 NLT

When you go through deep waters, I will be with you. When you go through rivers of difficulty, you will not drown. When you walk through the fire of oppression, you will not be burned up; the flames will not consume you.

"The Shield of God"

Today I pray…

Father, thank you, for when I am faced difficulties, You don't le go of me. You stand beside me as a shield against the winds an the waves. Your presence engulfs me. Every challenging dec sion becomes a decision of ease because You have given me th answer. All my answers are found in You. I seek to understan Your ways, not the ways of man. Thank you Father, for being consuming fire that burns away all defeat and that clears the wa for Your love to be revealed in everything that I do. I rise abov adversity, seeing the glimmering light shining bright before m serving as a torch of Your love. I settle my thoughts before Yo and mediate on Your goodness; the goodness of Your thought toward me and everything that You have assigned me to do thi day. I feel victory upon me because You are victory! Becaus Your Word says, "When you go through rivers of difficulty, you wi not drown." Hallelujah! I breath into Your Word and I exhale wit thanksgiving. I receive the benefits of Your promises for me thi day, in Jesus Name, Amen.

*Reflection*_____

_____

_____

Day 23

Philippians 2:14 AMP

*Do everything without murmuring
or questioning [the providence of God],*

"God's Word is True"

Today I pray…

Father, thank You for reminding me not to complain but to remain in a posture of thanksgiving. Everything that You have planned for me is done with purpose. You're intentional in everything that You do. There are no unanswered questions. You answered them all on the Cross. I meditate on Your Word according to Matthew 6:33 "But seek ye first the kingdom of God, and his righteousness; and all these things shall be added unto you." Today Father, I choose to be a truth seeker and not grumble or complain. For it is Your sovereign hands that rest upon my Life. A life filled with purpose and destiny. A life filled with leadership and servitude. A life filled with joy, peace, and love in every area of my life. I look for goodness in all circumstances because I know that is where You will be found. You are goodness and Your mercy endure forever! Thank You Father for Your unyielding love. I find hope in the assignment You have placed before me. The wind of change has blown my way. I receive the newness of what You're doing this day, in Jesus Name, Amen.

Reflection_____

_____

_____

Day 24

1 Corinthians 13:7 NLT

Love never gives up, never loses faith, is always hopeful, and endures through every circumstance.

"The Power of Love"

Today I pray…

Father, thank You, for Your love is alive in me! Your love keeps me. Faith and Hope are my anchor in every circumstance. I see the dawn of the day shining brightly before me. My expectations rise for what lies ahead. You are a God that seeks to lavish Your goodness upon his children. Your Word declares in Luke 11:13 "If ye then, being evil, know how to give good gifts unto your children: how much more shall your heavenly Father give the Holy Spirit to them that ask him?" Thank You Father for the gift of endurance. I choose to embrace this gift that You have graciously given me. When faced with uncertainty, It is Your love and kindness that performs and moves every situation into my favor. Thank You for favor; it rests upon my life and everything that is attached to me. My children, family, friends, employees and my leader are all favored. My love walk is being elevated as I receive the goodness of Your Word. I see the breaking of the dawn. Every crooked place has been made straight, in Jesus Name! Every obstacle has been destroyed. Love has taken the victory lap. I choose to join in the celebration this day, in Jesus Name, Amen.

Reflection_____

_____

_____

Day 25

Psalm 139:23 NLT

Search me, O God, and know my heart;
test me and know my thoughts.

"The Pureness of God's Love"

Today I pray…

Father, thank You, for my thoughts are always before You. There is nothing that is hidden from You. Your Word declares in Matthew 10:30 "But the very hairs of your head are all numbered." You see me, and You know me so well. Teach me Father to lead with a gracious heart. Allow my thoughts to stay pure before You. Father, give me wisdom to know when I fall into error and the heart to receive correction. I want my actions to be a reflection of Your character. Purify my heart and my thoughts. Purge me from all worldly thinking. Come Holy Spirit, You are welcome! Every thought that is a contradiction to Your Word is dismembered in Jesus Name! You have searched me and found me. My heartbeat is in sync with You. I decree and declare that I am in rhythm with Your heartbeat and my spirit leaps with joy this day, in Jesus Name, Amen.

Reflection_____

_____

_____

Day 26

Job 31:6 KJV

*Let me be weighed in an even balance
that God may know mine integrity.*

"A Leader of Honor"

Today I pray…

Father, I thank you that it is by integrity that leaders are established. It is Your sovereign hand that places leaders in position. Teach me Lord how to remain balanced in all areas of my life. Guide me in my speech and let my words be words of honesty. Let my actions be guided by Your movements of righteousness. Thank You for surrounding me with Your Holy presence. I give way to Your will. You justify because You are justice. All balances weigh in Your hands. I thank You for the integrity of my heart is before You. I ask that You take hold of my intertwining thoughts and that my leadership will serve as equal liberty to Your goodness. Your Word declares in Psalms 78:72 "So he fed them according to the integrity of his heart; and guided them by the skillfulness of his hands." Lord, let there not be any selfishness found in me. Let my love be for Your people that You have entrusted me to lead. You chose David, your servant, and You have chosen me from my hidden place. Thank You for Your gracious assignment and the ability to discern accurately. I receive this day with a humble heart and a spirit of expectation to lead in my full potential, in Jesus Name, Amen.

Reflection_____

_____

_____

Day 27

Proverbs 13:4 NLT

*Lazy people want much but get little,
but those who work hard will prosper*

"Be a Finisher"

Today I pray…

Thank You Father that my hunger to finish what You have started is greater than any obstacle standing before me. I arise with energy and excitement to search out Your days' plan. For it is Your goodness that rests upon my daily comings and goings. My agenda is full of Your distinct handprint and I see the written words before me. You're a God that reveals to those who are bold enough to seek Your Kingdom purpose. It is the Kingdom of God that wants to be revealed in the workplace through those who desire to be His carrier. Father, You declared in Your Word to the disciples in Luke 10:9 "And heal the sick that are therein, and say unto them, the kingdom of God is come nigh unto you." Lord, I pray that the people will be receivers of Your word through the Holy Spirit. Allowing the kingdom of God to be released in greater authority and power. Releasing prosperity over every word of accountability, encouragement, and correction. Thank You, for in this release is an abundance of creativity being formulated in my environment. Ideas that bring forth achievement, advancement, and excellence to the organization and all who are connected. Complacency is not connected to me nor the people whom I lead in Jesus Name. We work with skillful hands and a servant's heart. Always ready for what lies ahead because we know victory is the result, in Jesus Name, Amen.

Reflection_____

_____

Day 28

Proverbs 16:3 NLT

*Commit your work to the Lord, and
then your plans will succeed.*

"A Loyal Worker"

Today I pray…

Thank You Father, for I humbly commit my days' work unto you. I receive my daily bread, and I partake of Your wisdom. You have orchestrated every outline of my assignment, which is designed to succeed. You have filled in the blanks with Your love. It's that love that carries me through the day and brings delight. For I choose to delight myself in my work because commitment in You brings exuberance to my life and the life of others. Thank You Father, for Your love is contagious, Your joy is contagious! May the spirit of joy resonate throughout the workplace. I pray that Your people will set aside all vain ambitions and commit their life and their work to You. For Your Word declares in Psalm 127:1 "Except the LORD build the house, they labour in vain that build it: except the LORD keep the city, the watchman waketh but in vain." Lord, You are the Master Builder, the Teacher, and the High Priest. You are the keeper of all plans. Unless You be at the center, all work be in vain. Teach us Lord how to surrender to Your plans. Allowing You to establish a firm foundation and setting Your Word over our lives. I pray that eyes be open to the door made available through Your glorious riches, in Jesus Name, Amen.

Reflection_____

_____

_____

Day 29

Ecclesiastes 49:10 NLT

Two people are better off than one, for they can help each other succeed. If one person falls, the other can reach out and help. But someone who falls alone is in real trouble.

"Cooperating with God's Plan"

Today I pray...

Thank You Father, for You have given us a cloud of witnesses whom cheer us on! Let Your Kingdom come on earth as it is in heaven. Teach us the gift of teamwork. Celebrating one another in our successes and encouraging in our failures. Father, let it be seen that it is better for two than one when attempting to accomplish greatness. Help us understand the generosity of helping one achieve to ensure that the next achieves. Lord, I pray that compassion will fall upon Your people to be generous with their gifts, talents, and skills in the workplace. I decree and declare that unhealthy competition be nullified in Jesus Name and a gracious spirit be released into the atmosphere. Lord, allow a spirit of humility to take over the heart of Your people, and that an extension of kindness be extended to all those willing to receive. Father, let us be partakers of Your portion. Portions of courage, strength, and fierce determination for our fellow colleagues to be elevated in success. Allow a greater passion to comprehend that we are all promoted when we help each other succeed. Father, use me today to reach out, to be the hand that can be a lifter of a soul, in Jesus Name, Amen.

*Reflection*_____

_____

_____

Day 30

Job 5:9 NCV

God does wonders that cannot be understood; he does so many miracles they cannot be counted.

"The Miracle Worker"

Today I pray…

Thank You Father, for Your amazing love! Your love cannot be comprehended, nor can it be understood. My spirit receives the riches of who You are in me. You are the Father that never stops working on my behalf. When I feel inadequate, it's Your love and kindness that draws me back to You. It's in the wonders of Your presence that keeps me steady. Thank You for the miraculous miracles that are unfolding right now, the miracles that have yet to been seen, the miracles that are in motion, and the miracles that have already happened. You are a God of miracles! I step into my miracle, I surrender to every miracle, and I embrace every miracle that You have designed specifically for me. I do not question what I do not understand, but I trust Your process and purpose. My life is not my own for I trust You Lord. My faith gives way to Your plan. Your purpose for me is greater than the natural mind can comprehend, but my spirit receives it right now in Jesus Name! The miracles of heaven are available to me in this moment. The very breath I breathe is a miracle, and I praise Your Holy name. I remain in a posture of yes. Yes to Your will, Yes to Your way, and Yes to all Your wondrous miracles that surround me, in Jesus Name, Amen.

*Reflection*_____

_____

_____

Day 31

2 Corinthians 3:12 MSG

With that kind of hope to excite us, nothing holds us back.

"Released into Victory"

Today I pray…

Thank You Father, for You give me hope and that hope brings excitement to this journey. It's a journey with You. One that sustains me and strengthens me in all I do. There is nothing that can hold me back. For You have propelled me in the spirit and I have excelled to greater heights and deeper depths in You. Nothing holds me back! The assignment that is before me is complete with Your handprint. Success is upon me and excellence reigns over me. Integrity leads, wisdom navigates, and love carries me. Father, thank You that nothing can stand against Your will. I rest knowing that I sit in the palm of Your hand. All my ideas come from You. I have the mind of Christ, which produces God's ideas. Nothing can hold me back! My excitement is great, for I know the plans that You have for me. They are prosperous plans. It is a future with no end because in You, there is no end. Thank You for giving me a hope that anchors my love and sustains my faith. Nothing can hold me back! I move forward this day with excitement, expectation, and passion for what lies ahead. The journey is full of Your beauty and there are streams of joy and mountains of peace. Nothing can hold me back! You carry me, nothing can hold me back. Father, You carry me, and nothing can hold me back. My hope is in You, in Jesus Name, Amen.

*Reflection*_____

_____

_____

Resources

All Bible scriptures references are taken from Biblegatway.com
Zondervan Corporation.

CPSIA information can be obtained
at www.ICGtesting.com
Printed in the USA
BVHW030910110620
581279BV00001B/1